Patterns of the Earth

Bernhard Edmaier
Patterns of the Earth

With commentaries by
Angelika Jung-Hüttl

Introduction

From a purely geographical point of view, the surface of the earth is covered with rivers and lakes, mountains and valleys, glaciers, islands, coastlines, deserts and many other landscape elements. But if you look at our planet's richly textured crust from the perspective of an artist or a designer, it is made up of a diverse mixture of patterns. Some are very small, only a few millimetres in size, while others are many kilometres wide, so that they can only by recognized from the air. Rivers, for example, appear as winding ribbons, elongated parallel sand dunes as stripes, volcanoes as circles, islands as spots, fissures in a mountain or crevasse fields on a glacier as grids, the cracks in the dried-out mud of riverbanks as webs, and so on.

These structures are created by geological forces such as heat and pressure in the earth's interior, by volcanic activity and also by external forces that act upon the planet, such as weathering and erosion caused by sun, wind, water and glacier ice. Even the temperature differences between night and day or summer and winter gradually lead to the disintegration of the hardest rock. Wind, water and glacier ice break up and grind the rock, then carry the rubble away with them, often over great distances, and deposit it at a different location.

Only a few patterns on the surface of the earth are created by a single force, such as the circle of a crater pit, blasted from the subsurface during a volcanic eruption. The majority of patterns and structures are the result of the interplay of a number of different processes that can often happen over long periods of time, sometimes continuing for millions of years. For example, the heat and pressure of the earth's interior are required to create folding patterns in a rock mass: the high temperatures make the brittle rock strata malleable. The high pressures that occur during orogenesis (mountain building) folds them and pushes them up towards the surface. Wind, water and glacier ice then cut deep gorges and valleys into the mountains, like a knife cutting a slice from a layer cake. The folds in the mountain flanks and canyon walls now become visible. If the rock strata are not folded and bent during orogenesis, but fracture into blocks and are tilted instead, the original rock sequences are retained and appear in section as a parallel pattern of linear bands and stripes.

Some patterns are only visible from the air, like these mangrove-fringed river branches in the Ord River Delta, Western Australia

Top: first tectonic forces crack the limestone, then sediments fill the gap; erosion washes channels into tilted sediment layers; water meanders over a plain, always following gravity. Bottom: crater hole made by a volcanic eruption; salt circles deposited by underground springs; the thawing and freezing of permafrost creates stone rings

Completely different forces can often create very similar structures. For example, stripes can also occur when a number of glacier tongues carrying rubble towards the valley in extended ridges unite to form a single ice flow and continue to transport the debris in neighbouring lines. Ripples are not only created by the flow of water over sand on beaches or on riverbanks – the wind can also form ripples on an area of sand. Rainwater, flowing across inclined beds of limestone can, given time, carve out runnels and create rippled, wrinkled surfaces, known as limestone pavement. Even the course of a glacial outwash river, which meanders across an expansive plain, forms – when seen from a height of several hundred metres – a ripple pattern.

The colours of many of earth's patterns are due to the chemistry of the rocks, or to the mineral and suspended materials content of the water of seas, lakes and rivers. Red or yellow rock generally contains iron minerals, while green water conceals large amounts of algae. Milky grey glacial water is clouded by the fine dust scraped up from the rocks below and ground by the ice on its journey to the valley. Vegetation can also emphasize the patterns on the surface of the earth, for example in the form of a border of green palms along the ribbon formed by a desert river bed.

The earth's patterns possess an almost indescribable, mysterious sense of aesthetics. The reason for this may lie in the fact that these structures are created strictly in accordance with the laws of nature. Rivers or flowing glacier ice seek out the straightest route downhill, always following gravity's pull. Should they encounter an obstacle on the way, they will gnaw at it until they have either negotiated or eliminated it. Rock weathers most quickly in places where it is broken, or where its mineral composition allows it to be most easily dissolved by water. The famous photographer Andreas Feininger wrote in his book *Forms of Nature and Life* (1966): 'The forms of nature are functional. And precisely because they are functional, we find them beautiful.'

Below freezing point, water creates hexagonal crystals. Like tiny six-petalled flowers, hoarfrost covers snow layers after a very cold night

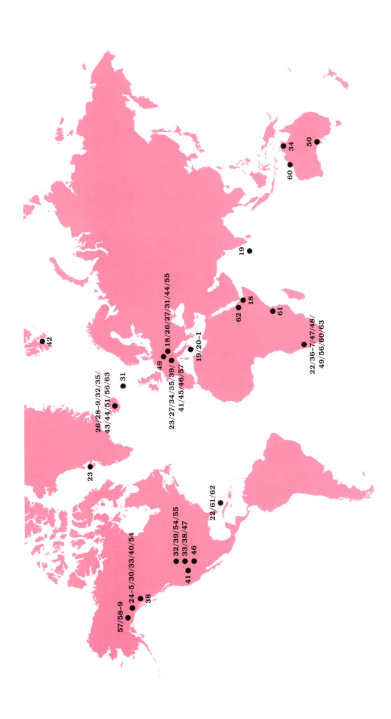

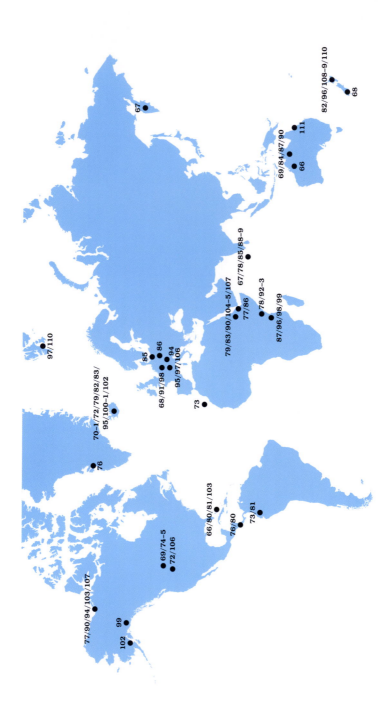

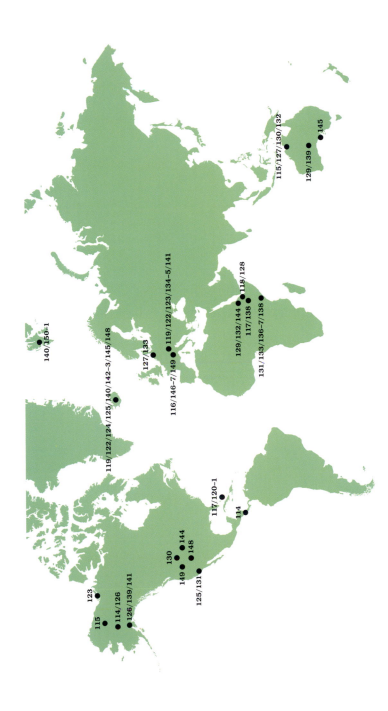

190

179/180–1/183

166

188

164

162–3

175

167/168/170–1/184

164

185

191

165

154/178

160/172–3/174/176–7/179/186–7

161/182/189

175/182

178

169

169/188

167/174

156–7

158/159

166

183/185/190/191

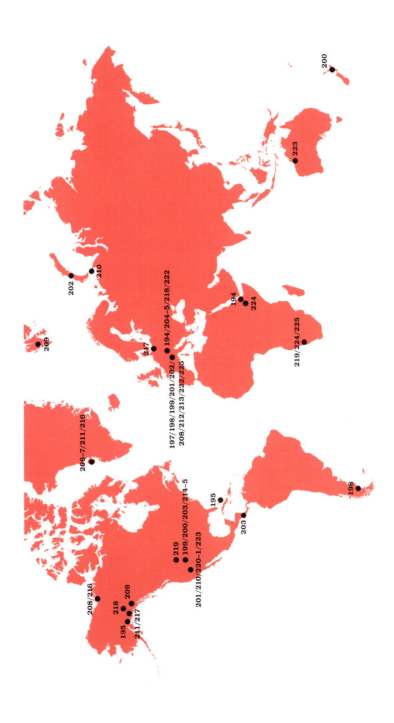

Bands
Stripes
Ripples

Wooded promontory in the River Inn on the German-Austrian border

Watery filaments in a desert valley, Sac Allol, Djibouti, Africa

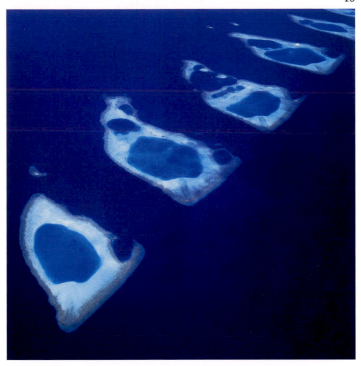

Chain of reef islands on the edge of the Ari atoll, Maldives

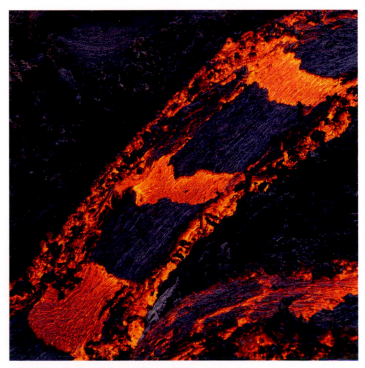

Minor lava flow on Mount Etna, Sicily, Italy

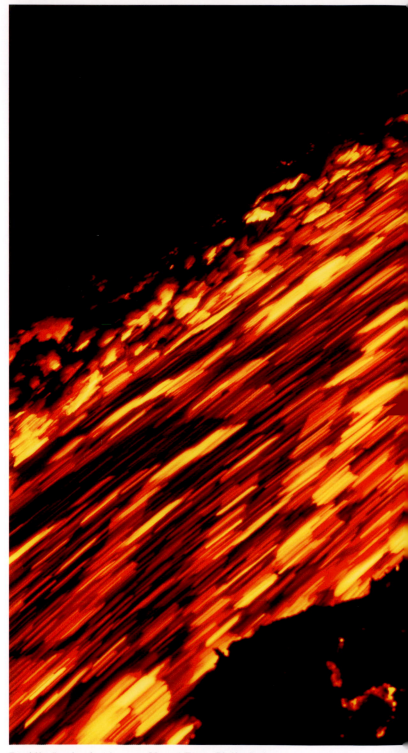

Rapidly flowing hot lava on Mount Etna, Sicily, Italy

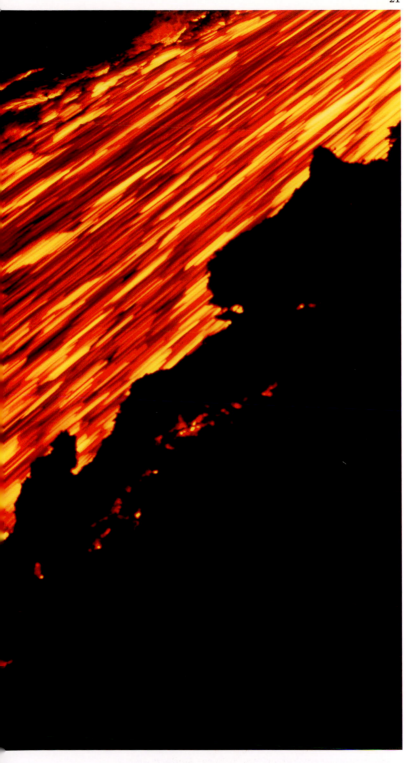

Crest of a linear dune, Namib Desert, Namibia, southwest Africa

Boundary between shallower and deeper sea bed, Bahamas

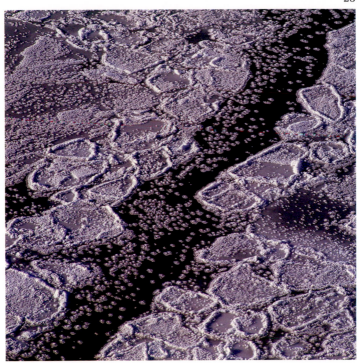

Open water between ice floes in Qeqertarsuup Tunua (also known as Disko Bay), Greenland

Meltwater channel, Gauli Glacier, Bernese Oberland, Switzerland

Ice wall at the front of Hubbard Glacier, Alaska, USA

Red joint fill in pale limestone, Steinernes Meer, a plateau in the Bavarian Alps, Germany

Waterfall tumbling over basalt columns, Svartifoss, Iceland

Moraine strip on the furrowed Aletsch Glacier, Valais, Switzerland

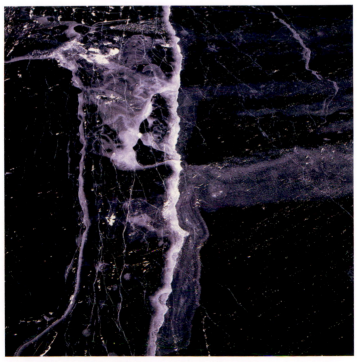

Fracture zone in ice on Lake Silvaplana, Graubünden, Switzerland

Hard lava layer in a mossy mountainside, Ljóttipollur, Iceland

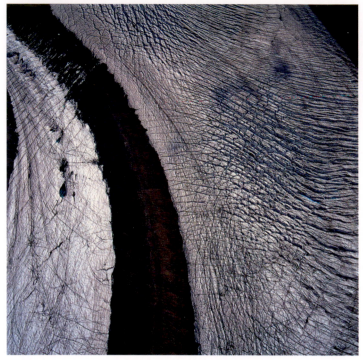

Strip of moraine debris on Russell Glacier, Alaska, USA

Sandy beach and mangrove swamps in the Gulf of Tadjoura,
Djibouti, Africa

Side arm of the River Inn on the German-Austrian border

Mykines, Faroe Islands, Denmark

Algae-covered water channel on a sinter crust, Yellowstone National Park, Wyoming, USA

River valley in Landmannalaugar, Fjallaback, Iceland

Sandstone weathering formations, Paria Wilderness, Utah, USA

Ice tongue of Kluvesna Glacier, Wrangell Mountains, Alaska, USA

Mangrove belt parallel to the coast, Northern Territory, Australia

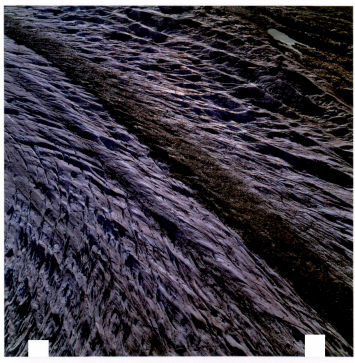

Moraine debris on Finsteraar Glacier, Valais, Switzerland

Meltwater channel beside a beach ridge of dark volcanic sand,
Skeidarársandur, Iceland

Moraine debris on the ice of Aletsch Glacier, Valais, Switzerland

Parallel linear dunes in the Namib Desert, Namibia, southwest Africa

Channels on the flank of an iceberg, Tracy Arm Fjord, Alaska, USA

Cross bedding in a sandstone formation in Zion National Park, Utah, USA

Runoff channels in the ice wall above a lake on Gorner Glacier, Valais, Switzerland

Tilted strata near Sheep Mountain, Bighorn Basin, Wyoming, USA

Bands of debris on the ice of Malaspina Glacier, Alaska, USA

While slowly creeping downhill, glacier ice carries all
the debris from rockwalls that has fallen onto its surface
forward like a conveyor belt, leading to the formation
of straight-edged stripes of moraine rubble. When a
number of glacier tongues meet in one big ice mass like
the Malaspina Glacier in Alaska, these moraine stripes
are laid close together (above). In the Badlands near Las
Vegas, Nevada, runoff water has cut gullies and valleys
into the tilted multicoloured sediment layers, resulting in
a pattern of yellow and reddish bands (bottom right). The
pattern of the irregular banded gneiss of the Verzasca
River bed in Ticino, Switzerland, was caused by the high
pressure and temperature conditions in the deep interior
of the earth (top right). Light-coloured layers are rich in
lucid minerals like quartz and feldspar, dark layers
contain more black mica like biotite.

Gneiss in the bed of the Verzasca River, Ticino, Switzerland

Multicoloured strata, Badlands near Las Vegas, Nevada, USA

Snow-covered erosion channels on Wallenbergfjellet, Spitsbergen,
Svalbard archipelago

Erosion ravines covered by alpine grassland on the Dialer Polen,
Trentino-Alto Adige, Italy

Basalt columns in the gorge of Aldeyjarfoss waterfall, Iceland

Icicles on Schleier Falls, Bavarian Alps, Germany

Rock wall of basalt columns, Svartifoss, Iceland

Steep erosion ravines on Hohen Ifen, Allgäu Alps, Germany

Rock ribs above La Creta, Valais, Switzerland

Crevasses in Obere Ischmeer Glacier, Bernese Oberland, Switzerland

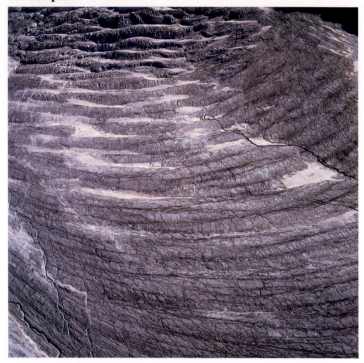

Ogives or flow ridges in the Ewigschneefeld (eternal snow field),
Aletsch Glacier, Valais, Switzerland

Variegated strata in the Painted Desert, Colorado Plateau, USA

Erosion formations in sandstone, Paria Wilderness, Utah, USA

Sand dunes in the Namib Desert, Namibia, southwest Africa

Volcanic deposits containing iron on Reykjanes Peninsula, Iceland

Mountain ridges and valleys cut by a river, Damara Mountains, Namibia, southwest Africa

Layers of lighter and darker volcanic ash, Eifel, Germany

Dune field in the Namib Desert, Namibia, southwest Africa

Multicoloured clay layers in the bed of a stream, Arkaroola,
South Australia

Ogives hemmed in by moraine bands, Gilkey Glacier, Alaska, USA

Moraine and volcanic ash formations in the ice of Skeidarárjökull, southern Iceland

Bands of moraine debris on Malaspina Glacier, Alaska, USA

Tilted strata in the Damara Mountains, Namibia, southwest Africa

Rock strata on Sheep Mountain, Bighorn Basin, Wyoming, USA

Moraine banding on Steller Glacier, Alaska, USA

Folded salt layers, Berchtesgaden salt mine, Bavarian Alps, Germany

Mountainside furrowed by erosion channels in the Badlands of
Bighorn Basin, Wyoming, USA

Dune field in the Namib Desert, Namibia, southwest Africa

Grey glacier water and yellow bog water on Landeyjarsandur coastal plain, Iceland

Earth ridges in a dry string bog, Monahan Flats, Alaska, USA

Crevasses filled with snow from the previous winter on Tsanfleuron Glacier, Valais, Switzerland

Dried out watercourses in a swamp region, Clearwater Mountains, Alaska, USA

Sand ripples on the dunes of Sossusvlei, Namibia, southwest Africa

Current formations in the tidal zone of Roebuck Bay, Western Australia

Large ripples in the shallow ocean near Long Island, Bahamas

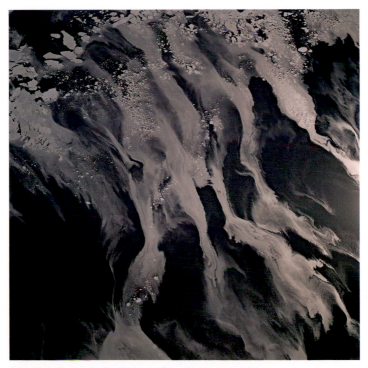

Salt streaks on Lake Natron, Tanzania, east Africa

Salt precipitation on Lake Afrera, Denakil Desert, Ethiopia, Africa

Underwater dunes in the shallow ocean near Long Island, Bahamas

Sand dunes dissipating into rock desert, Namib Desert, Namibia, southwest Africa

Fissures above Grímsvötn, a subglacial volcano, Vatnajökull, Iceland

Circles
Spots
Grains

Blue hole, entrance to a submarine karst cave, Bahamas

Wolfe Creek crater, meteorite impact site, Western Australia

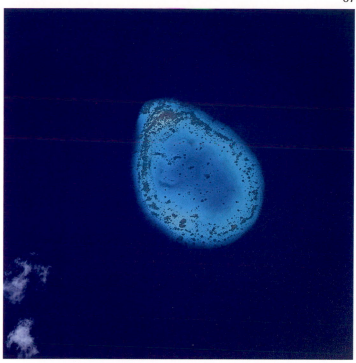

Small reef island with lagoon in the centre, Baa Atoll, Maldives

Acid crater lake, Maly Semiachik volcano, Kamchatka Peninsula, Russian Federation

Meltwater tunnel, Franz Josef Glacier, South Island, New Zealand

Feldsee, a tarn in the Black Forest, Germany

Morning Glory Pool, hot water pool, Yellowstone National Park, Wyoming, USA

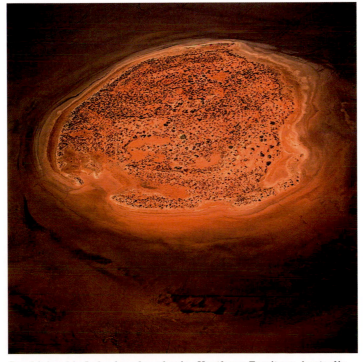

Sand island in Lake Amadeus basin, Northern Territory, Australia

Relict volcano covered with common water moss on
Mælifellssandur, Iceland

Upheaval Dome, sinkhole above subterranean salt, Utah, USA

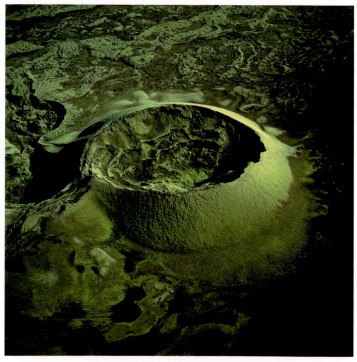

Ancient, moss-covered volcanic crater on Laki Fissure, Iceland

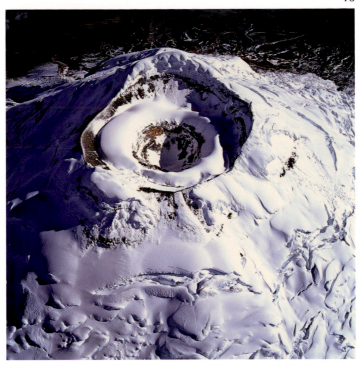

Crater of the glaciated volcano Cotopaxi, Ecuador, South America

Caldera de los Cuevos (Raven Crater), volcanic cone on Lanzarote, Canary Islands, Spain

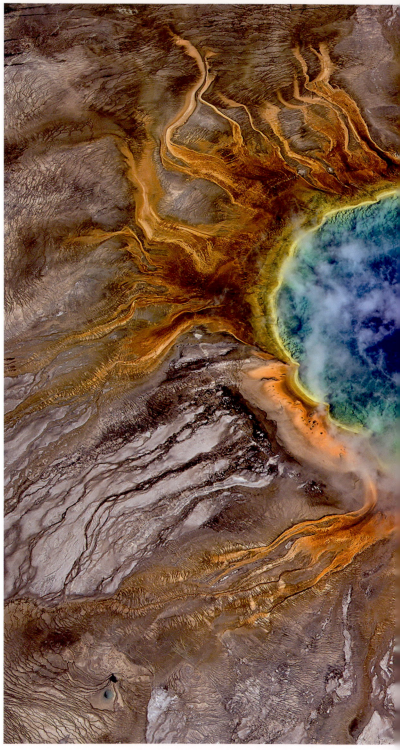

Grand Prismatic Spring, hot water spring, Yellowstone National
Park, Wyoming, USA

Acid crater lake on the volcano Poás, Costa Rica, Central America

Meltwater lake on an iceberg in Ilulissat (also known as Jakobs-havn), Greenland

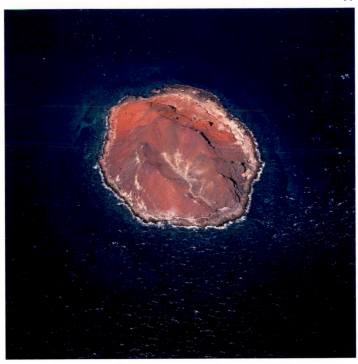

Island in the Les Sept Frères group off the coast of Djibouti, Africa

Ibyuk, pingo or frost mound in permafrost in the Mackenzie Delta near Tuktoyaktuk, Canada

Lake Paradise, a crater lake in the Marsabit National Reserve,
Kenya, Africa

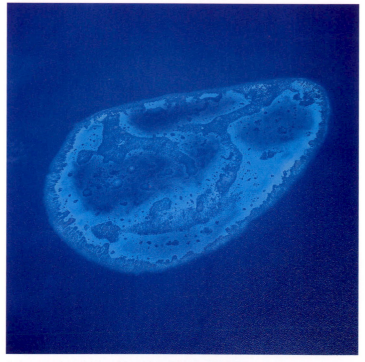

Submerged reef island in the Ari Atoll, Maldives

Volcanic crater, Denakil Desert, Ethiopia

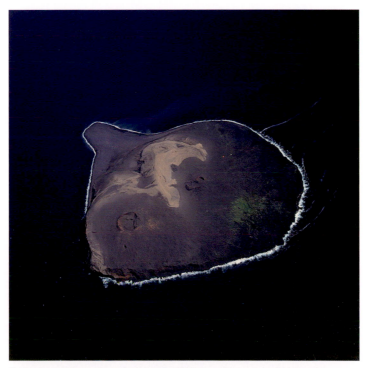

Surtsey, young volcanic island off the south coast of Iceland

Acid lake in the crater of Rincón de la Vieja volcano, Costa Rica, South America

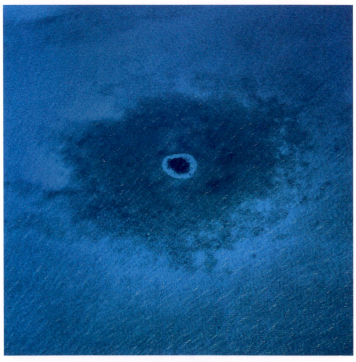

Coral stock in the shallow ocean near New Providence, Bahamas

Quilatoa crater lake in the highlands of Ecuador, South America

Blue Hole, entrance to an undersea cave, Bahamas

Meltwater lake on Vatnajökull Glacier, Iceland

Champagne Pool, hot spring with orange algae fringe, Waiotapu, North Island, New Zealand

Hill covered with moss on Mælifellssandur, Iceland

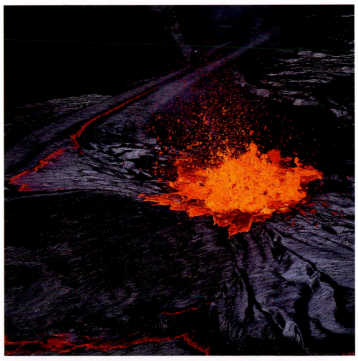

Hot, glowing fountain on the lava lake in the crater of Erta Ale volcano, Ethiopia, Africa

Sand island in Lake Amadeus, Northern Territory, Australia

For a variety of often highly complex reasons, small islands frequently have a rounded shape. The sand island in Lake Amadeus, a salt lake in the Australian desert, is only an island during the rainy season, when the lake basin is filled with water (above). During dry periods, it is a low, barely visible hill on the floor of the lake basin. The sand was originally accumulated by the wind. The rounded shape of this hummock is the result of the constant interaction of irregular winds, transporting sand from different directions, and the lake currents during the rainy season. The circular structure is retained by the plants that now grow on the island and stabilize the sand with their roots.

The currents along Germany's Baltic coast are responsible for the circular structure of the two round islets of the Werder Islands, which form part of a coastal moor (top right). Reed beds buttress the edges of these salt meadow islands, stabilising their shape.

The cause of the round structure of the Ari Atoll reef islands in the Maldives lies under water (bottom right). A sunken volcanic mountain range, with innumerable large and small summits, rises from the ocean floor. Corals and sponges populate these peaks, their calcium carbonate skeletons building up the ring-like reef.

Werder Islands, Vorpommersche Boddenlandschaft National Park, eastern Germany

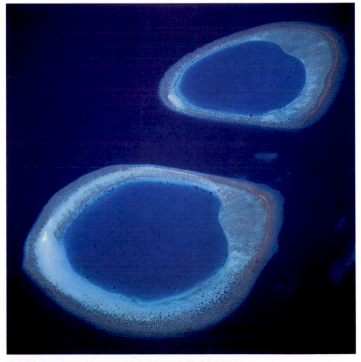

Reef islands in the centre of Ari atoll, Maldives

Low sand hills in the lake basin of Grand Barra Depression, Djibouti, Africa

Densely forested islands in Lake Wumm, Brandenburg, Germany

Deposits around the saline springs in the swamps of Lake Natron, Tanzania, Africa

Sand islands in the almost dry Lake Amadeus, a salt lake, Northern Territory, Australia

Circular reef islands in the centre of South Male Atoll, Maldives

Erosion holes in the sandstone of Uluru (Ayers Rock), Northern Territory, Australia

Salt crust in the geothermal region of Dalol, Ethiopia, Africa

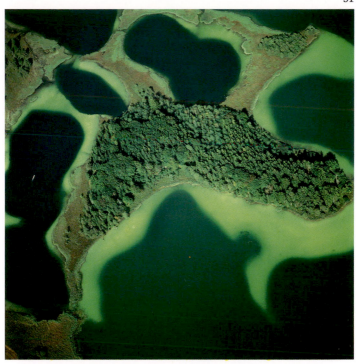

Basins between the small islands in Großer Ostersee, a lake in southern Germany

Lake landscape in the permafrost of Mackenzie Delta, Canada

Salt formations in the sand of Chalbi Desert, Marsabit, Kenya, Africa

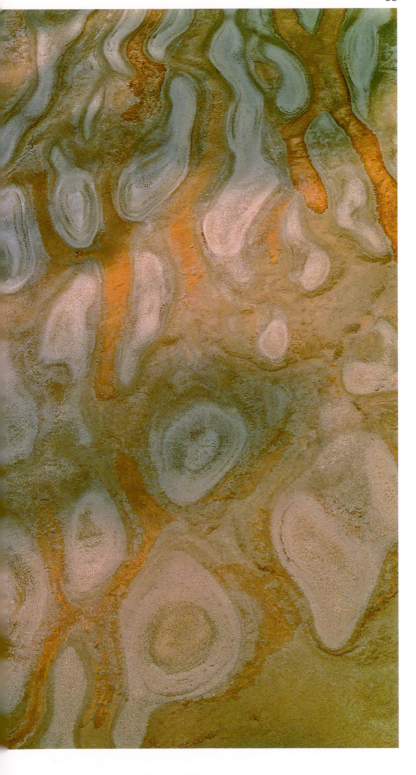

Hochstegen Marble, abraded by glacier ice, Zillertal Alps, Austria

Pingo or frost mound in the permafrost of Mackenzie Delta, Canada

Volcanic ash deposits in the ice of Hofsjökull Glacier, Iceland

Individual air bubbles in the ice cover on Lake Silvaplana,
Graubünden, Switzerland

Small soda salt springs in the salt swamps of Lake Natron, Tanzania, Africa

Mud pool with bubbles of volcanic gases, Waiotapu, North Island, New Zealand

Stone polygons on the coastal plain of Isfjorden, Spitsbergen, Svalbard archipelago

Fields of bubbles in ice on Lake Silvaplana, Graubünden, Switzerland

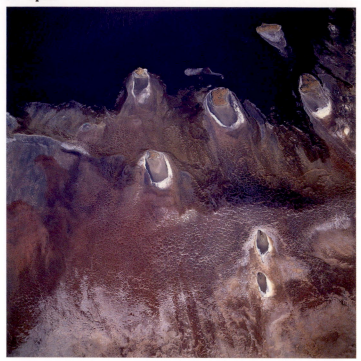

Islands at the edge of Lake Natron's salt swamps, Tanzania, Africa

Limestone islands in Eibsee, a lake in southern Germany

Kettle lakes in the debris-strewn ice of Malaspina Glacier, Alaska, USA

Soda salt springs close to the swampy shore of Lake Natron, Tanzania, Africa

Crater field on the peninsula in Lake Mývatn, northern Iceland

Green lakes on the debris-strewn ice of Lateral Glacier, Aleutian Range, Alaska, USA

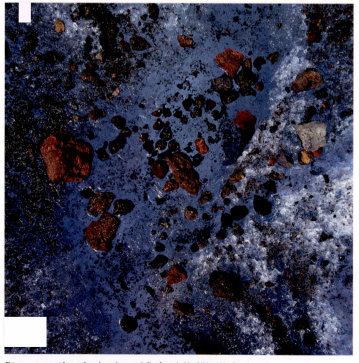

Stones on the glacier ice of Svínafellsjökull, Iceland

Coral stocks in the shallow ocean near New Providence, Bahamas

Beaded streams in the tundra near Shingle Point, Canada

Degassing vents in a sinter crust in the geothermal region of Dalol,
Ethiopia, Africa

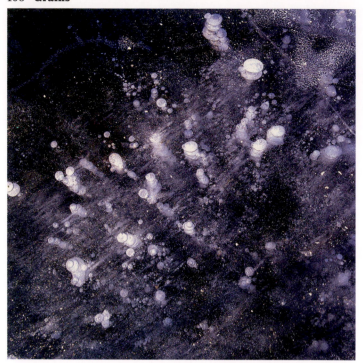

Air bubbles in ice on Lake Silvaplana, Graubünden, Switzerland

Globular weathering formations in sandstone, Paria Wilderness, Utah, USA

Salt crust containing iron hydroxide minerals in Dalol, Denakil
Depression, Ethiopia, Africa

Polygons in the tundra of the Mackenzie Delta, Canada

Gas bubbles in volcanic mud at Hell's Gate, North Island,
New Zealand

Stone polygons on the permafrost of Isfjorden, Spitsbergen, Svalbard archipelago

Gas bubbles in volcanic mud at Hell's Gate, North Island, New Zealand

Pseudo craters in the moss-covered lava field of Eldhraun, Iceland

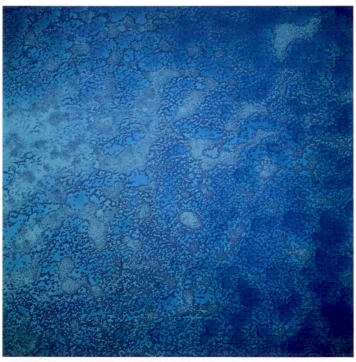

Limestone formations in the Great Barrier Reef near Cairns, Queensland, Australia

Forks
Branches
Webs

Flow-induced beach forking, Playa Marino Ballena, Costa Rica, Central America

Lateral inflow on Ruth Glacier, Denali National Park, Alaska, USA

Confluence of two water arms in the Yukon Flats, Alaska, USA

Fork in the Ord River Delta fringed by mangroves, Western Australia

Confluence of Grenz Glacier and Gorner Glacier, Valais, Switzerland

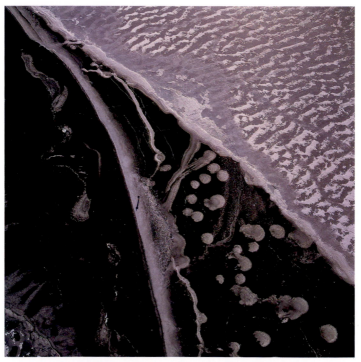

Fractures in partially snow-covered ice on Lake Silvaplana, Graubünden, Switzerland

Water network in the Awash River flood plain in Ethiopia, Africa

Current channels between the islands of the Exuma Cays, Bahamas

Dried out, partially salt-covered drainage channel near Lake Assal, Djibouti, Africa

Algae streaks in Lac Abbé, a saline lake, Djibouti, Africa

Confluence of a stream stained yellow by iron minerals in Thjórsá River, southern Iceland

Mixture of river and lake water of differing opacity in Lake Constance, southern Germany

Tidal channel near Long Island, Bahamas

Erosion channels filled with snow, Landmannalaugar, Iceland

Mouth delta of the Tiroler Achen river into Chiemsee, a lake in southern Germany, in summer

Mouth delta of the Tiroler Achen river into Chiemsee, a lake in southern Germany, in winter

Widely branching arms in the Mackenzie Delta, Canada

Glacier water on Skeidarársandur on the south coast of Iceland

Flowing water often creates dendritic patterns on the
earth's surface. The surface topography is crucial to
this process. Obeying gravity, water always tends towards
lower-lying areas and then collects at the lowest point.
On wide plains it can spread along numerous arms and
will sometimes fill and cover entire regions — such as
the sediment-loaded, and therefore opaque, meltwater
that flows in huge quantities from Iceland's glaciers. It
forms large, shallow lakes on the sand plains between
the mountains and the coast, before collecting in channels
and flowing to the sea (above). In contrast, the water in
a river stained yellow and orange by iron minerals splits
into a multitude of channels where it opens into the sea
(top right).

     In semi-desert regions, where rain only rarely falls,
water flows through erosion channels towards the larger
river valleys and collects there. Pale-coloured salts,
which remain after the water has evaporated, clearly
trace the routes taken by the water on the brown desert
floor (bottom right).

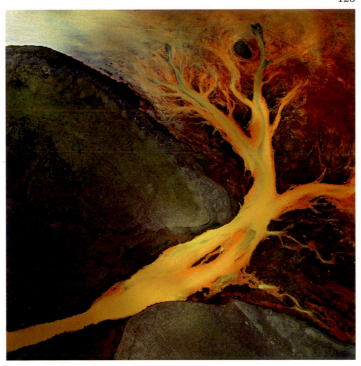

River mouth on the Landeyjarsandur on the south coast of Iceland

Dried out watercourses with salt deposits, Carrizo Plain, California, USA

Water arms on Susitna Flats flood plain, Alaska, USA

Tidal channels coloured red by algae in a bay in Cook Inlet, Alaska, USA

River system fringed by mangroves in the Ord River Delta,
Western Australia

Tidal channels in the salt meadows of the island of Mellum, North
Sea coast, Germany

Streaks of algae in the water of Lac Abbé, Djibouti, Africa

Runoff channels on the salt crust at Allol, Djibouti, Africa

Fractures in the crust of the lava lake on Erta Ale volcano, Denakil Desert, Ethiopia

Dried-up river beds in the Painted Desert, South Australia

Tidal channels fringed by mangroves in the Ord River Delta,
Western Australia

Water channels in the sinter crust of a hot spring, Yellowstone
National Park, Wyoming, USA

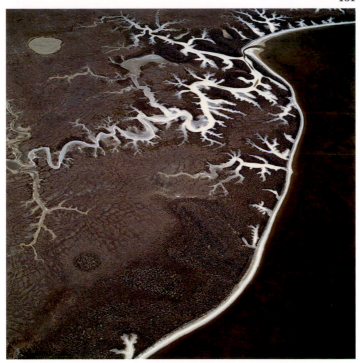

Pale-coloured river network and lakeshore on Carrizo Plain,
California, USA

Delta of the Engare Ngiro river in the swamps of Lake Natron's
northern shore, Kenya, east Africa

Dried-out watercourses on the edge of the Denakil Desert,
Ethiopia, Africa

Mangroves and salt deposits in the Ord River Delta, Western Australia

Drainage channels on the eastern sand flats of the island of
Spiekeroog, North Sea coast, Germany

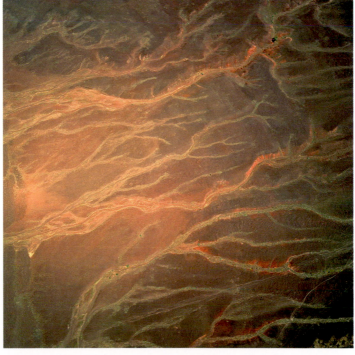

Dried-out water courses west of Lake Turkana, Kenya, east Africa

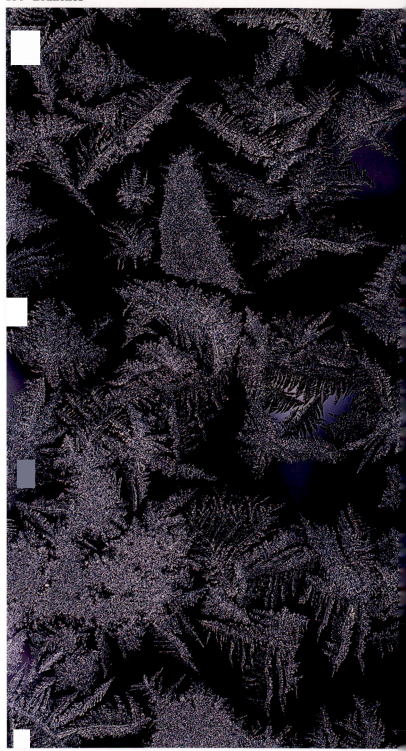

Frost flowers on a window, Pleiskirchen, southern Germany

Rows of bushes along dried-out water channels, Chalbi Desert, Kenya, east Africa

Water channels in a flood plain of the River Awash, Ethiopia

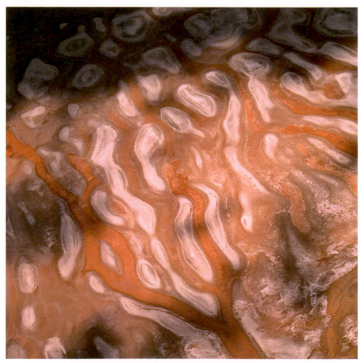

Erosion channels in the salt crust on Chalbi Desert, Kenya, east Africa

Grass-covered levees in a string bog on Chitina River, Cook Inlet, Alaska, USA

Sand dunes in the desert near Uluru (Ayers Rock), South Australia

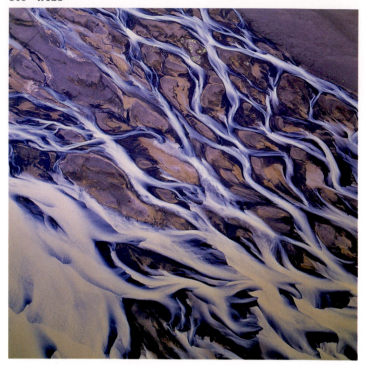

Glacier water flows on Skeidarársandur, Iceland

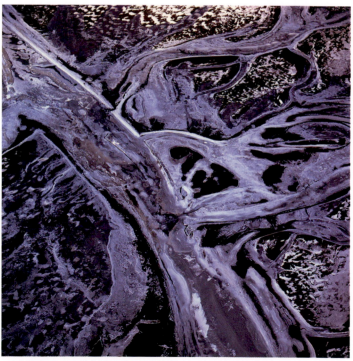

Frozen riverbeds in Kjellströmdalen, Nordenskiöldland,
Spitsbergen, Svalbard archipelago

Arms of the River Isar near Vorderriß, Bavarian Alps, Germany

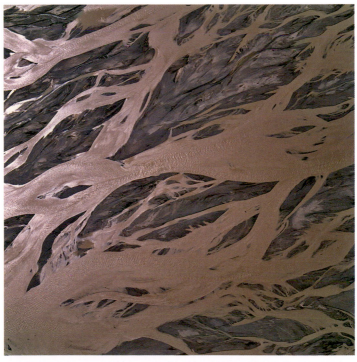

Sandbanks surrounded by water in the Chitina River, Alaska, USA

Glacier stream network on Skeidarársandur, Iceland

Massive quartz veins in the rocks of Black Canyon of the Gunnison National Park, Colorado, USA

Dried out water channels in the Denakil Desert, Ethiopia, Africa

Web of innumerable watercourses on Skeidarársandur, Iceland

Dark deposits in the basin of Lake Torrens, a salt lake, South Australia

Network of fractures in ice on Lake Silvaplana, Graubünden, Switzerland

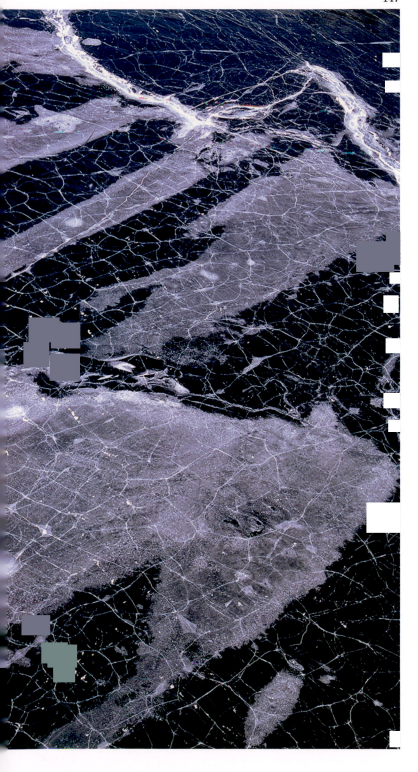

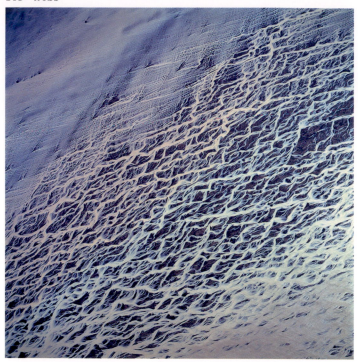

Dense network of glacier streams on Skeidarársandur, Iceland

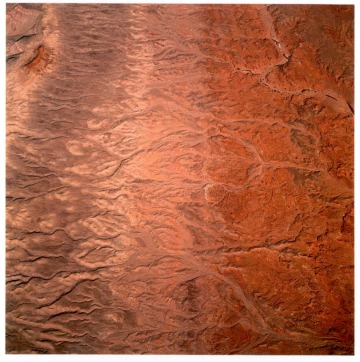

Erosion channels on Kaibito Plateau, Arizona, USA

Sandstone mountains near Lake Mead, Nevada, USA

Network of fissures on Trift Glacier, Valais, Switzerland

Widely branched meltwater channels on a tongue of Negribreen
Glacier, Sabineland, Spitsbergen, Svalbard archipelago

**Curves
Ribbons
Swirls**

Ice tongue with moraine bands, Aletsch Glacier, Valais, Switzerland

Valley cutting through the edge of the Kimberley Plateau,
Western Australia

Bank of the South Alligator River, Northern Territory, Australia

Reef edge in the sea off Conception Island, Bahamas

Ogives on Gilkey Glacier, Coast Mountains, Alaska, USA

Moraine bands on Russell Glacier, Saint Elias Mountains, Alaska, USA

Small debris bands on Klutlan Glacier, Saint Elias Mountains, Alaska, USA

Moraines bent by the flow of ice, Malaspina Glacier, Alaska, USA

Moraine patterns on Malaspina Glacier, Alaska, USA

Boundary between sand desert and the Atlantic Ocean, Namibia, southwest Africa

Large, uniformly curved lines are not often seen on the surface of the earth. These shapes are usually created by complex geological processes acting on the planet's surface, but occasionally they are simply the result of geometry. The coast bordering Namibia's sand desert (above) forms a huge arc at this point because of the region's surface topography. It is nothing more than the intersection between the ever-level surface of the sea and the undulating surface of the neighbouring sand desert.

The Svínafellsjökull glacier tongue in the south of Iceland creeps toward the valley, obeying the laws of gravity. There, it meets a river valley and bends accordingly to follow the gradient. The many deep fissures in the surface of the glacier (top right) are an indication of the enormous tensile and compressive forces generated inside the ice.

The broad sweep of this reef edge in the Great Barrier Reef on Australia's east coast is formed by ocean currents (bottom right).

Ice tongue of Svínafellsjökull, Iceland

Great Barrier Reef near Cairns, Queensland, Australia

Volcanic cone intersected by lava flow, Sugata Valley, Kenya, east Africa

Großer Werder, promontory on the Baltic Coast of Mecklenburg-Vorpommern, Germany

Coastal channels filled with seawater, Khor Angar, Djibouti, Africa

Sandbank curved by current off Long Island, Bahamas

Tidal channels in the North Sea tidal flats off the island of
Pellworm, Germany

Bow in the Yukon River, Alaska, USA

Watercourses in the Ord River Delta, Western Australia

Meandering river in the Mackenzie Delta, Canada

River arms in the Oder valley near Schwedt, eastern Germany

River Kösseine in the Fichtelgebirge, southeast Germany

Meandering Tollense River, eastern Germany

San Juan River Canyon, known as Goosenecks, Utah, USA

Dry riverbed, tributary of Little Colorado River, Arizona, USA

Small stream winding through meadows, Bavarian Forest, southeast Germany

Loops in Fishriver Canyon, Namibia, southwest Africa

Meandering stream in the coastal plain west of the Mackenzie Delta, Canada

Boundary between rock and sand desert, Kuiseb River, Namibia, southwest Africa

Garlands of salt crusts on the shore of Lake Natron, Tanzania, east Africa

Sand bars in the shallow sea of the Bahamas, near Eleuthera

Dune crests in the Namib Desert, Namibia, southwest Africa

Meltwater channels and lake on Gorner Glacier, Valais, Switzerland

Tunnel in the ice of Perito Moreno Glacier, Patagonia, Argentina

Channels in the brackish water landscape of Alligator River, Northern Territory, Australia

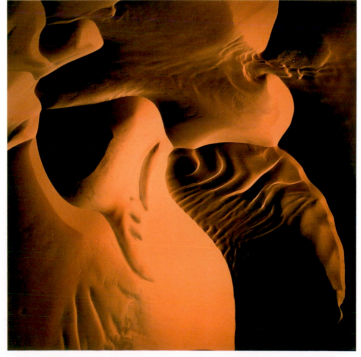

Pyramid dune with rippled flanks in the Namib Desert, Namibia, southwest Africa

Layered rock hills in the Bungle Bungle Range, Purnululu National
Park, Western Australia

Volcanic ash formations in the ice of Skeidarárjökull, Iceland

Underwater sandbanks off a small island near Eleuthera, Bahamas

Water channels in a closed basin or endorheic depression, Kakadu
National Park, Northern Territory, Australia

Fresh, cooling lava crust, Kilauea, Big Island, Hawaii, USA

Ice formations on a gurgling spring, River Isen, southern Germany

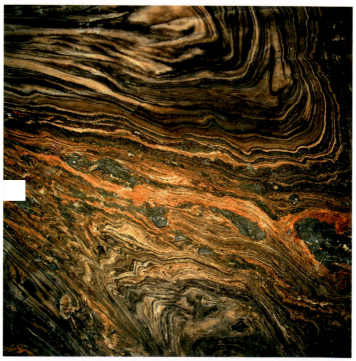

Folds in saline rocks, Berchtesgaden salt mine, Bavarian Alps, southern Germany

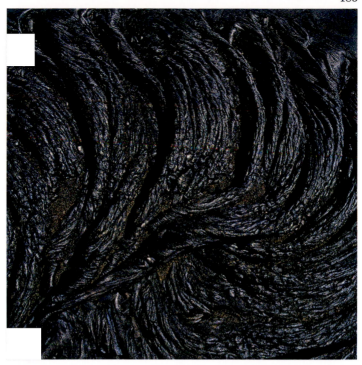

Strings of pahoehoe (ropy lava), Kilauea, Big Island, Hawaii, USA

Striped gneiss polished by high water in the bed of the River
Verzasca, Ticino, Italy

Erosional valleys in the horizontal layers of the Huns Mountains,
Namibia, southwest Africa

Weathered sandstone, Gantheaume Point, Western Australia

Erosional channels in mineral-rich, clayey rocks of the Kaibito Plateau, Arizona, USA

Dry volcanic mud, Krísuvík, Iceland

Volcanic soil coloured by minerals, Reykjanes Viti, Iceland

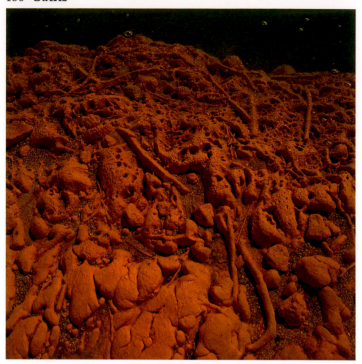

Sinter crust covered by algae on the edge of Champagne Pool, North Island, New Zealand

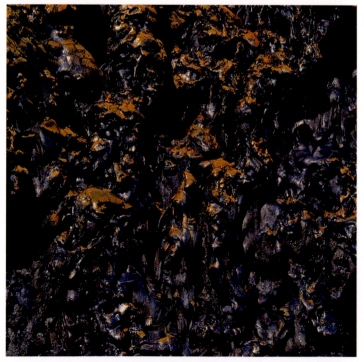

Crust of extremely low viscosity lava, Kilauea Caldera, Big Island, Hawaii, USA

Fractured, speckled pahoehoe (ropy lava), Kilauea, Big Island, Hawaii, USA

Sulphur deposits around the main crater of Mount Etna, Sicily, Italy

Spikes
Grids
Cracks

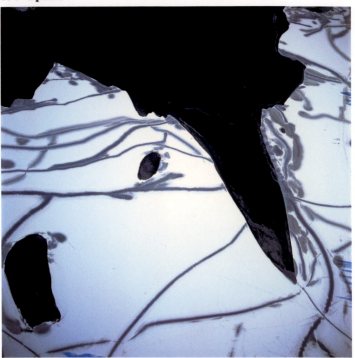

Fractured ice on Großer Ostersee, a lake in southern Germany

Narrow rib of rock protruding into the sea, Ghoubbet el Kharab, Djibouti, Africa

Pointed sandbank near Long Island, Bahamas

Ice towers on Columbia Glacier, Alaska, USA

Earth pyramids near Soprabolzano, Trentino-Alto Adige, Italy

Ice towers at the front of Perito Moreno Glacier, Argentina

Earth pyramids near Soprabolzano, Trentino-Alto Adige, Italy

Rock columns in Bryce Canyon, Utah, USA

Rupturing front of Fiescher Glacier, Bernese Oberland, Switzerland

Sulphur needles on a volcanic gas vent, Waiotapu, North Island, New Zealand

Rock formations in the Needles District, Canyonlands National Park, Utah, USA

Ice towers on Aletsch Glacier, Valais, Switzerland

Eroded salt crust in Badwater, Death Valley, California, USA

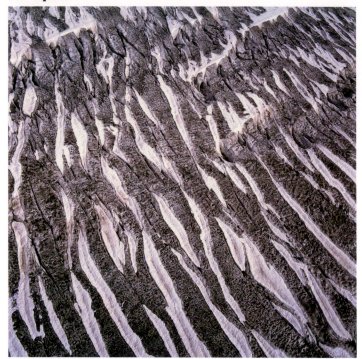

Snow-filled fractures in the ice of Tsanfleuron Glacier, Valais, Switzerland

Heavily fissured glacier in Inostranzeva Bay, Novaya Zemlya, Russian Federation

Ribs of rock in the Needles District, Canyonlands National Park, Utah, USA

Erosional formations in the crater wall of Irazú volcano, Costa Rica, Central America

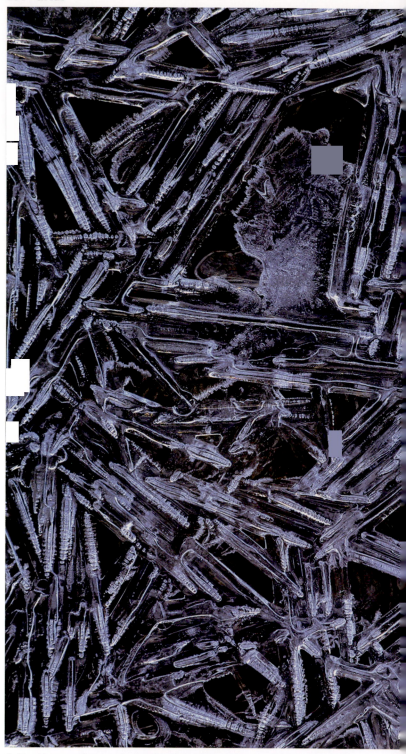

Grid of ice needles on the banks of the River Isen, southern Germany

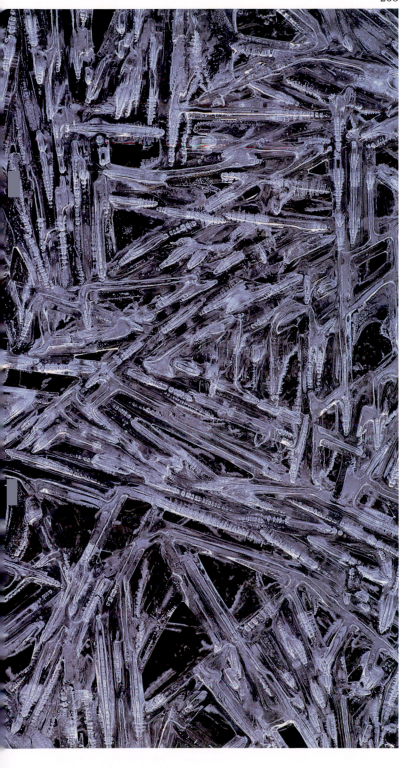

Freshly fractured sea ice cover in Qeqertarsuup Tunua (also known as Disko Bay), Greenland

Permafrost tundra showing polygons, Shingle Point, Canada

Fractures in the ice cover on Lake Silvaplana, Graubünden, Switzerland

Polygon patterns in permafrost in Agarddalen, Spitsbergen, Svalbard archipelago

Troughs in the ice of Hubbard Glacier, Alaska, USA

Polygons in the permafrost on Vaygach Island in the Arctic Sea, Siberia, Russian Federation

Polygons in the salt crust in Badwater, Death Valley, California, USA

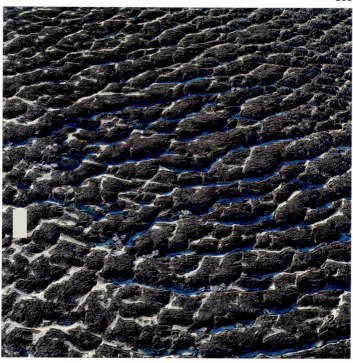

Fissures filled with meltwater on Bering Glacier, Alaska, USA

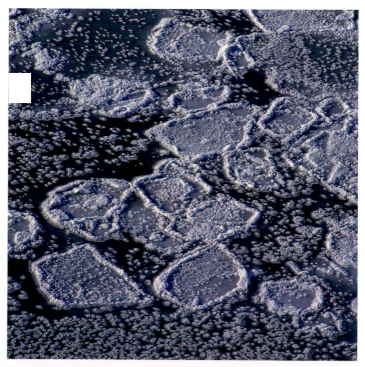

Pancake ice in the waters of Qeqertarsuup Tunua (also known as Disko Bay), Greenland

Crevasse pattern on Zwillings Glacier, Valais, Switzerland

When glacier tongues creep towards the valley, fissures form in the ice. Depending on the gradient, speed of flow and roughness at the base of the glacier, the ice fractures either at right angles, parallel or diagonally to the direction of ice flow. This gives rise to a variety of grid structures.

Fissures divide the surface of the Zwillings Glacier (above) into angular ice blocks. The Aletsch Glacier — at 23 kilometres overall length the longest glacier in the Alps — displays a number of different lattice patterns. In the higher regions, around the area of what is known as the Aletschfirn (Aletsch névé), temperatures rarely climb above freezing point, even in summer. Here, the snow from the previous winter that fills the fissures does not melt away, but remains, tracing the tracks of the fissures (above right). Further down valley, where it is warmer and the terrain becomes steeper, the fissures expand (bottom right). Now, the uppermost layer of ice on the glacier tongue can completely disintegrate. Ice towers and peaks are the result.

Crevasses filled with old snow on Aletsch Glacier, Valais, Switzerland

Deeply fissured ice field on Aletsch Glacier, Valais, Switzerland

Grooves and channels in the sandstone of Checkerboard Mesa, Zion National Park, Utah, USA

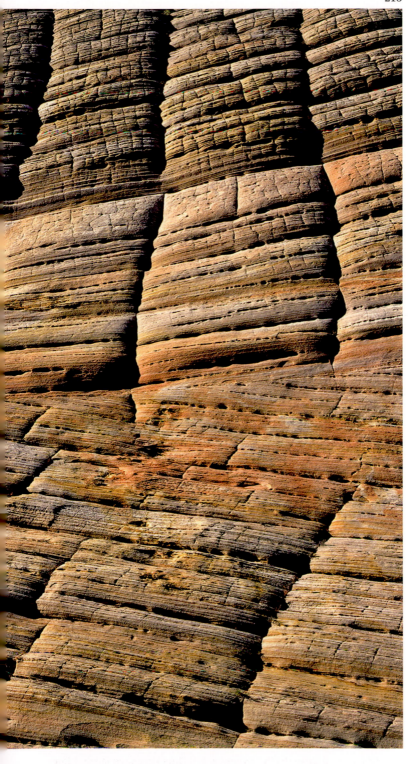

Polygon soil in permafrost near Shingle Point, Canada

Icebergs in Ilulissat (also known as Jakobshavnfjord), Greenland

Channel network in coastal bog on Kir Peninsula, Mecklenburg-Vorpommern, eastern Germany

Icebergs in a meltwater lake at the front of Bering Glacier, Alaska, USA

Icebergs in a meltwater lake at the front of Nizina Glacier, Alaska, USA

Fracture lines in the limestone of Gottesacker Plateau, Allgäu Alps, southern Germany

Joint network in slate, Naukluft National Park, Namibia, southwest Africa

Sinter terraces, Mammoth Hot Spring, Yellowstone National Park, Wyoming, USA

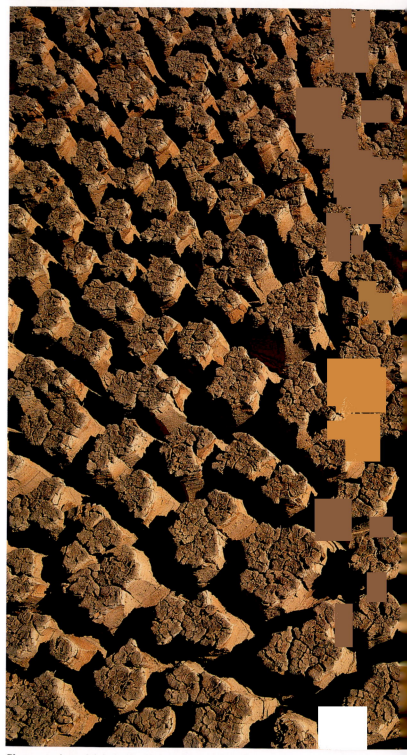

Close-up view of dried silt, Mojave Desert, California, USA

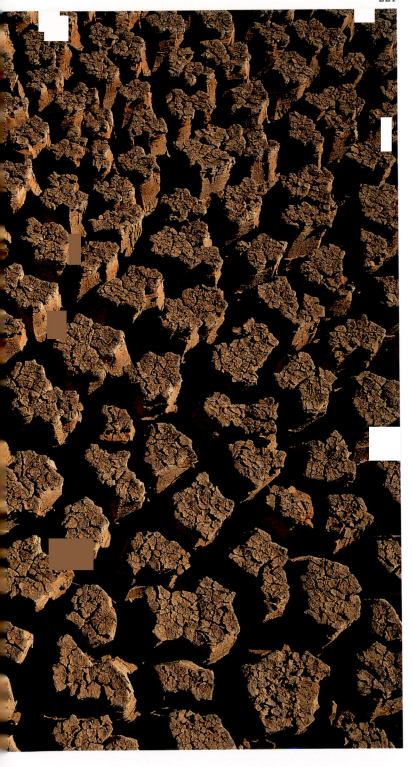

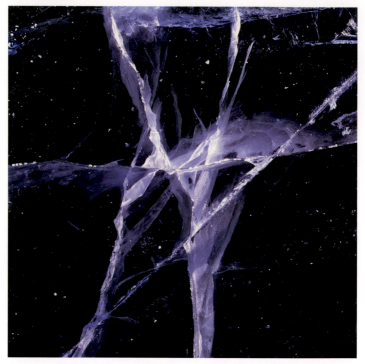

Fractures in ice on Lake Silvaplana, Graubünden, Switzerland

Fractures in limestone rock in the Untersberg south face, Bavarian Alps, southern Germany

Fractured sandstone on the coast near Gantheaume Point,
Western Australia

Joint network in quartzite rocks, Death Valley, California, USA

Dried salt crust, Dalol, Ethiopia

Cracks in dried mud in the bed of the Swakop River, Namibia, southwest Africa

Shards of dried mud, partly covered with salt, Swakop River, Namibia, southwest Africa

Fracture in the ice cover of a glacier cave, Findelen Glacier, Valais, Switzerland

Glossary

Algae
Aquatic green, brown or red photosynthetic plants that inhabit both salt and fresh water. There are more than 25,000 species, ranging in size from microscopic single-cell diatoms to giant kelp tens of metres long.

Basalt
Dark, fine-grained volcanic rock, created when liquid lava rises from the depths of the earth. As it cools down, the molten rock sometimes splits into a series of separate polygonal surfaces, and solidifies into five- or six-sided basalt columns.

Caldera
A large depression, at least 1.5 kilometres wide, formed at the end of a large volcanic eruption, when the top of a volcano collapses into its empty magma chamber. The word comes from the Spanish for 'cauldron'.

Carbonate
In purely chemical terms, carbonates are the salts of carbonic acid. Some kinds of carbonate are among the commonest rock-forming substances on earth. Limestone, for example, consists of calcium carbonate (chemical formula $CaCO_3$). It is chiefly deposited in

sea water. If CO_3 combines both with calcium and magnesium, it produces dolomite.

Coral reef
Structures of calcium carbonate built by coral animals on coasts between 30 degrees north and south of the equator. In order to develop, they need very clean, shallow sea water, a great deal of light, and a water temperature between 20 and 30 degrees Celsius.

Crater
Round depression created through impact on the earth's surface or eruption of a volcano.

Crater lake
Lake formed when rainwater collects in the crater of a volcano. When corrosive volcanic gases escape under water, it becomes an acid lake.

Cross-bedding
Internal structure of dunes or stream deposits. Horizontal sand beds show tilted or inclined fine layers. Fossil cross-bedding structures can allow scientists to determine the directions of winds or currents millions of years ago, when the sediments were deposited.

Delta
Fan-shaped sedimentary deposit of silt or clay that forms above water level when a river flows into a lake or sea. When the still water of a lake or the waves of the sea act as a brake on the flow of the river, the floating particles carried in the river sink to the bottom. The river delta pushes its way further and further into the main body of water with the constant addition of further sediment.

Doline
Bowl- or funnel-shaped depression in karst regions, with round or elliptical outline and a diameter ranging from one to many hundreds of metres. Commonly called a sinkhole, a doline develops when the roof of a karst cavern becomes unstable because of the corrosive solution of rainwater and collapses.

Flood plain
Portion of the river valley that is made up of sediments and is repeatedly inundated with water. In tropical and subtropical regions such flooding occurs during the

rainy season, while in glacier regions it is caused by shifts in temperature.

Flue
Channel or system of tubes reaching many kilometres underground, through which glowing magma spills up from the earth's interior to the surface, and is expelled through a crater (see **Volcanic vent**). After a phase of eruption the flue fills with stones and is gradually blocked by cooling lava – until it is blown open again with the next eruption.

Frazil ice
The freezing of sea water begins with the formation of semi-soft individual ice crystals on its surface. These fine needles and plates, up to four millimetres in diameter, initially float independently of one another on the water, before multiplying and gradually coming together to form grease ice.

Fumarole
Volatiles escaping from vents in the surface of lava flows and around the craters of volcanoes through which generally sulphurous, pungent-smelling gases and steam pours out. The gases can reach a temperature of 1,000 degrees Celsius. (see **Precipitate**).

Geothermal spring
Spring from which warm water, often high in mineral content, emerges out of the depths of the earth. As it cools down, the minerals are precipitated and deposited in a siliceous (or calcareous) sinter crust around the spring basin. If the water is hotter than human body temperature (37 degrees Celsius) it is called a 'hot spring'; if it ejects boiling water and steam it is termed a geyser.

Glacier
Ice mass that forms on land surfaces in cold climatic regions, where temperatures are so low for most of the year that snow collects regularly. Over time the layers of snow turn into ice under their own weight. Ice behaves plastically, so glacier tongues in the mountains creep down towards the valleys. There are three main types: valley glaciers are confined to a path that directs their movement; piedmont glaciers break through these channels and move out over level ground, while ice sheets move outwards in all directions from the start.

Gneiss

One of the metamorphic rocks, most of which are very old, their original structure and composition transformed by extremely high pressure and temperatures within the earth. Gneiss is distinguished by its coarse-grained, layered texture, with different minerals arranged in parallel lines. Its main components are feldspar, quartz and mica.

Grease ice

The second stage in the freezing of sea water, which occurs when frazil ice crystals join together. For this to occur, a calm surface is required.

Ice field

Network of connected glaciers. Unlike individual glaciers, which often start in a hollow between individual mountain peaks, ice fields cover a whole massif.

Karst

Highly fissured limestone landscape, often riddled with caves. These underground caverns are produced when rainwater, which always contains a small quantity of carbonic acid, corrodes the calcium carbonate. Over time it washes out underground caves. Strata of rock that are rich in the mineral gypsum can also become karst.

Lava

As soon as magma, the hot molten rock within the earth's interior, reaches the surface during the eruption of a volcano, it is termed 'lava'. It can flow out into streams or blow apart into fine particles, described as volcanic ash, which can rise several kilometres into the air as an ash-cloud. Lava generally has a temperature between 1,000 and 1,200 degrees Celsius. The rock formed when it solidifies is also called lava.

Limestone

Umbrella term for rocks consisting of carbonates, most of them made up of calcium and magnesium carbonate. They often contain fossils and shell fragments.

Meander

Bend in the course of a river flowing along a flat surface. Meanders are formed when the level ground slows down the water as it pushes its way forwards. As a result, the river settles into a series of loops.

Mica
A group of lustrous sheet silicate minerals found, for example, in granite and gneiss. Mica comes from the Latin word 'micare', meaning 'to shine'.

Moraine
Rocky material that has been smoothed down, carried away and deposited by glaciers. This rubble consists of a great variety of debris – from blocks the size of houses to the finest clay particles.

Ogive
Convex bulge on the surface of a glacier tongue, arising at the foot of a steep slope in the ice, and caused by seasonal differences in the motion of flow. The ice creeps more quickly towards the valley in the summer than in the winter because of the higher temperatures.

Pancake ice
With wave swell, the grease ice on the sea's surface breaks down into pancake ice, countless circular floes that collide with one another and are thicker at the edges as a result.

Permafrost
In very cold regions (arctic, subarctic, alpine), where temperatures remain below zero almost all year round, the subsoil is always frozen. The upper layers thaw only in the summer, forming vast marshes. Permafrost underlies roughly 20 per cent of the earth's surface, and can vary in depth from 30 centimetres in milder climates to more than 1,000 metres in some regions of Siberia.

Pingo
Small hill in the flat tundra landscape of permafrost regions. Pingos form when lakes dry up or drain, and the water-saturated soil under the former lake freezes slowly. The expanding ice pushes up the soil until a volcano-like cone appears. This process takes hundreds of years. Pingos can reach a height of more than 40 metres.

Precipitate
A solid forced out of a liquid or from vapour as the result of a chemical reaction or a change in temperature or pressure. When the water from geothermal springs, high in mineral content, emerges at the surface of the earth and cools, the minerals separate from it and form crusts (see **Siliceous sinter**, **Fumarole** and **Geyserite**).

Pseudo crater
A round depression in a lava field. Pseudo craters occur when molten lava flows over marshland, leading to massive bursts of steam that leave behind circular craters similar to small volcanic craters. However, pseudo craters don't have a vent to the earth's interior.

Schist
Large group of rocks that have experienced extreme pressure during tectonic movements in the earth's crust, for example, in the formation of mountain ranges. This is reflected in their internal composition; they are foliated in appearance, and flake into thin plates.

Sedimentation
The process by which particles are precipitated either through water or wind or as the result of a chemical process. For example, the debris carried by rivers settles on the sea floor; wind sifts the sand, and can even pile it into dunes; and calcium carbonate is deposited in the water of warm sea basins.

Silica
Minerals consisting of silicon and oxygen. They occur in at least nine different forms. The commonest of these is quartz.

Sinter
Precipitation out of mineral saturated, and often hot, water. The deposit is found as thin coating or as a thick layer or crust, for example around hot springs.

Siliceous sinter
White, porous silica incrustation precipitated by geothermal springs and geysers.

Strata
Sediment or rock layers, also called beds. A stratum has internally consistent characteristics which differ it from the layers above and below. A stratum can be anywhere between a few millimetres to a kilometre or more in thickness.

Tributary
Any stream that feeds water to a larger river, which in turn flows into the sea.

Tundra
Level or undulating treeless region, poor in species, in
the sub-polar climatic regions (Arctic tundra) and in high
mountains (alpine tundra). The subsoil in these areas
is permanently frozen (see **Permafrost**). The transitional
zone between treeless tundra and the major forest areas
is known as 'wooded tundra'.

Volcanic ash
See Lava

Volcanic gases
Volcanoes emit fumaroles (sulphur gases) and dangerous
carbon dioxide, a colourless, odourless gas that is so
heavy it drives the oxygen out of the layers of air closest
to the ground, and can lead to suffocation.

Volcanic vent
Opening in a volcano from which glowing streams of lava,
ash-clouds or gases have emerged, or are still actively
emerging (see **Flue**).

Volcano
A vent in the earth through which magma and gases
emerge. Volcanoes with a central vent are usually conical
in shape. Those with several centres of eruption or an
eruptive fissure resemble an elongated massif.

Index

The photographer would like to express his thanks to the pilots who circled the same motif time and again, with great skill and endless patience, and always brought him safely back to earth; the scientists who showed him how the earth has evolved and how it works; the rangers who helped him in the national parks and nature reserves; the expedition organizers who stood helpfully by him in the extreme regions of the earth; the photographic developers who ensured the best possible development of his pictures; his colleagues for their stimulating, sometimes difficult, but generally fruitful discussions; and to Sara De Bondt, Paul McGuinness, Sue Medlicott, Alex Stetter and Amanda Renshaw, whose enthusiasm made this book possible.

Phaidon Press Limited
Regent's Wharf
All Saints Street
London N1 9PA

Phaidon Press Inc.
180 Varick Street
New York, NY 10014

www.phaidon.com

First published 2007
© 2007 Phaidon Press Limited

ISBN 978 0 7148 4679 8

A CIP catalogue record for this book
is available from the British Library.

Translations by Alan Johnson
Designed by Sara De Bondt
Printed in China